How to CARE FOR YOURSELF — WHEN YOU'RE A CAREGIVER for someone else

— A Life Guide —

How to CARE FOR YOURSELF — WHEN YOU'RE A CAREGIVER for someone else

— A Life Guide —

Dr. Suzanne Gelb, PhD, JD

FIRST EDITION

All rights reserved. This book or any portion thereof may not be reproduced or used in any manner whatsoever without the express written permission of the publisher except for the use of brief quotations in a book review.

Copyright © 2019 Dr. Suzanne J. Gelb, Ph.D., J.D.

Manufactured in the United States of America.

ISBN-13: 978-1-950764-08-2
ISBN-10: 1-950764-08-7

www.DrSuzanneGelb.com

PRAISE FOR... THE LIFE GUIDES

I wrote this life guide on handling the challenges of being a caregiver, as well as 10 other life guides on various topics, to help readers successfully navigate some of life's trickiest challenges.

Each Life Guide includes educational information sourced from my three+ decades of coaching and counseling in the field of emotional wellness.

What Readers Are Saying

Praise

I enjoyed your Caregivers Guide. It is appealing, well-organized and has great information.

—Dr. Mary Clark, PhD, psychologist

Dr. Gelb's "How to Care for Yourself Life Guide" is brilliant, helpful and so necessary.

Having myself been a caretaker four times, I can tell you that the last thing someone needs is one more overwhelming thing to do. You are already operating in a complete state of overwhelm and yet still need some support and an outlet.

Suzanne has created the perfect easy, but powerful. way to do something for yourself. The question prompts with fill-in-the-blanks, makes doing the work feel like a pleasurable outlet. Through her questions and suggestions it's as if she's walking along side you gently guiding you with her big, open, nonjudgemental heart.

If you are feeling the need for something supportive, but feel like you can't deal with even one more thing, this guide is a super gentle, but powerful way, might just be the answer.

—Tracy Baum-Finkel

Before, self-care wasn't a word I ever would have used — it felt selfish and indulgent... but after working through this guide, I see how easily I can make myself feel better — and how that helps me take better care of my loved ones.

I absolutely loved how this guide broke everything down, step by step. I never felt overwhelmed.

—Rebecca Rapple

"Learning how to love yourself and treat yourself kindly — even when your life, career, body, and relationships aren't 'totally perfect' — is one of the hardest things to do.

Dr. Suzanne Gelb breaks down the art of self-love into practical steps. No woo-woo vagueness. Just easy-to-follow exercises pulled from her 28-year career in the field.

If you're looking for practicality and effectiveness, these Life Guides are a steal of a deal."

—Susan Hyatt, Master Certified Life Coach, Published Author

"Your guidebooks are gems."

—Alexandra Franzen, Published Author, Writing Teacher

CONTENTS

Disclaimer   xiii

INTRODUCTION

Change How You Care for Yourself, Change How You Care for Somebody Else.   1

WHAT'S INSIDE AND HOW TO USE THIS GUIDE   4

STEP 1

What Are You Feeling?   5

STEP 2

What Are Your Limitations?   10

STEP 3

Manage Your Feelings.   15

STEP 4

Finding More Support.   23

STEP 5

Finding Satisfaction and Honor.   30

STEP 6

Creating a Self-Care Plan.   37

STEP 7

Understanding Positive Submission.   44

A FEW FINAL WORDS

Making Your Own Wellbeing a Priority Prevents Caregiver Burnout.   53

MORE TIPS, MORE TOOLS

5 FAQs About Stressful Caregiving Situations.   55

WHAT'S NEXT

Resources… to Keep Learning and Growing.   93

ABOUT THE AUTHOR   98

OTHER BOOKS BY THE AUTHOR   99

INDEX   101

DISCLAIMER

This book is a tool that can help you become the best caregiver you can be.

This book contains educational exercises and tips drawn from my career in the field of emotional wellness with over 30 years of experience. This book is for informational purposes only, and is not intended to diagnose or treat any illness, nor is it a substitute for professional or psychological advice, diagnosis, or treatment. Always consult a qualified health care professional before engaging in any new, self-help resource (such as this one) and with questions you may have about your health and wellbeing.

Any case material that may be alluded to in this book, including in articles, or in interviews [see Resources section] does not constitute guarantees of similar outcomes for the reader. No results can be promised, since everyone's personal development path is unique. Names and details have been changed for privacy.

Links inside this book to external websites are for informational purposes only. Linking does not imply endorsement of or affiliation with that site, its content, or any product or service it may offer.

All link URLs in this book are current at the time of printing. Link URLs may fail at some point if the page has been deleted or moved. The author assumes no responsibility or liability for broken links.

This concludes the disclaimer portion of this book.

Thank you. Enjoy this Guide ... and enjoy your life.

INTRODUCTION

Change How You Care for Yourself, Change How You Care for Someone Else

Welcome to The Life Guide on How to Care for Yourself When You're Caring for Someone Else.

If you picked up a copy of this Guide, chances are, you might be feeling ...

- **Grief** about the fact that somebody you love is sick, dealing with a disability, or otherwise unable to care for themselves without help.

- **Guilty** because you don't feel "privileged" and "honored" by your position as a caregiver.

    And there's nobody you can admit that to.

- **Resentful** because of the way this whole situation is affecting your life, draining your finances, or "holding you back."

- **Impatient** because things don't seem to be improving.

    And they might not ... ever.

- **Exhausted**, run-down, full of pent-up emotion or just ... so ... sad.

Whether you're a professional caregiver or someone who's had the position thrust upon them, being a caregiver is like enrolling for an accelerated Ph.D. program in **Patience** and **Compassion**.

It can be:

An incredible "spiritual training course" —

if you let it.

It can help you cultivate more empathy —

if you let it.

Or,

It can feel:

Agonizing, disruptive and meaningless —

if you let it.

In this Guide, you'll learn:

How to step into your role as a caregiver with deep love — learning how to take better care of yourself, as you care for others.

Let's begin.

What's Inside and How To Use This Guide

Inside this Life Guide, you'll find a series of steps to help you handle the challenges of being a caregiver in a way that:

— **Honors the person you're caring for**

and

— **Honors yourself.**

Some steps include fill-in-the-blank worksheets.

Other steps contain detailed tips and tactics to help you **process your feelings healthily**.

Each step is designed to help YOU **become the best caregiver you can be**.

The Contents page of this Life Guide gave you a peek at what's ahead.

STEP I

What Are You Feeling?

As a life coach and as a psychologist, I almost always begin my sessions, in either modality, with a simple emotional "check-in," to help the people I work with to connect with their feelings.

Why do we start there?

Because:

It's difficult to manage your feelings and release pent-up feelings in a safe, appropriate way when you may not know what those feelings actually are.

So let's do that now, with **a writing exercise** to **get all those feelings out** on the page.

Try not to:

- **Over-think** your answers

or

- **Worry if…**

They sound:

- "Too mean"

or

- "Too inappropriate"

Self-criticism is never OK.

Just express whatever you feel.

When I think about my role as a caregiver: (fill in the blanks)

Most of the time, I feel

_____

_____

_____

_____

*On **"good days"** I feel*

_____

_____

_____

_____

*On **"lousy days"** I feel*

_____

_____

_____

_____

*I'm so **tired of trying** (and not succeeding) to*

_____

_____

_____

_____

*I'm so **mad at myself** for*

_____

_____

_____

_____

*I'm so **mad at the person I'm caring for**, because*

_____

_____

_____

_____

*I'm so **mad at the doctors** / the laws and rules / the insurance providers / the system, **etc.,** because*

_____

_____

_____

_____

*I'm so **worried** about*

_____
_____
_____
_____

*This whole **situation makes me feel***

_____
_____
_____
_____

Naming your feelings isn't the same as "managing" them — but it's the first step.

We'll talk about **what to "do" with those feelings**, a bit later in this Guide.

Next:

Let's talk about **what you can control**, as a caregiver, and **what you can't**.

In other words: your *limitations*.

STEP 2

What Are Your Limitations?

You are a human being. You have certain limitations. Some things are **within your control** — and **others are not**.

The **person you're caring for** also has **limitations**. But their limitations are **different** from yours.

— They may have much less control over their body and mind.

— They may have less strength, less dexterity, or a diminished ability to process and retain information.

— They may need a great deal more help, just to get through the day.

Both of you are trying to do the best you can, with the unique set of abilities and limitations you both have.

The big difference is ...

Being of sound body and mind, you can learn to improve.

The person you're caring for may not have that same privilege.

By considering your limitations — and theirs — you can begin to build more **empathy** for the person in your care.

Try this writing exercise to help you understand your power and your limits. (fill in the blanks below.)

Just like before,

— Try not to **over-think** your answers

or

— **Judge** them.

Your only job here is to **be honest with yourself**.

I can't always control

_____

_____

_____

_____

but I can do

_____

_____

_____

_____

I don't always have the power to make

_____

_____

_____

_____

happen as fast as I'd like,

but I can still

_____

_____

_____

_____

I can't always stop

_____

_____

_____

_____

from happening,

but I can control how I respond. I can approach the situation with

_____

_____

_____

_____

I can definitely do

_____

_____

_____

_____

with more patience than I have in the past.

I definitely need more help and support when it comes to

_____

_____

_____

_____

I definitely have enough love and kindness within me to

_____

_____

_____

_____

Now that you have a better understanding of what's within your control, and what's not, let's talk about:

One thing that is VERY much within your control:

Learning to manage your feelings so that they don't get pent up and expressed negatively. (Like verbally "lashing out" at the person you love.)

STEP **3**

Manage Your Feelings

As a caregiver, it's essential to find healthy outlets for your feelings (especially anger).

When left unattended, **negative emotions can build** like steam in a tea kettle — there's so much heat, so much steam, until finally, all that energy has to go somewhere.

Unfortunately, for many caregivers, that "somewhere" translates into **verbally "lashing out"** at the person you're caring for.

At other times, this looks like **turning all that pain and anger inward, against yourself** —

For example,

— **Over-eating** to suppress emotions,

— **Drinking too much** to "calm down and numb out,"

— **Developing ulcers,**

or

— **Elevated blood pressure.**

All of these examples signify **a lot of emotional stress**, when left unattended and unexpressed.

It doesn't have to be this way.

And in a moment, we'll talk about…

How to manage those feelings in a healthy way.

But first, just to drive the point home, here is a story about:

What can happen when a caregiver doesn't know how to release negative emotions — like anger and resentment — in safe, appropriate ways.

Fred's 82-year-old mother was frail and vulnerable, and depended on him to meet most of her basic needs, especially because she had memory difficulties.

Fred loved his mother deeply, but he was frustrated by her limitations:

"You should know better than to turn up the heating pad when I had it on low!"

Fred's mother had difficulty meeting his expectations and unreasonable demands.

This caused his frustration to build. So much so, that when he saw his mother trying to stand up without her cane, he slapped her and yelled,

"What's wrong with you, you imbecile! You should know better than to get out of your chair without using a cane. Next time, I'm going to ignore you and let you fall!"

This dynamic is at the root of much abuse because, like Fred —

Many caregivers let their frustration build up over time, until it finally erupts in angry verbal and / or physical outbursts.

Physical abuse includes **inflicting physical pain or injury,** such as slapping or bruising.

Emotional abuse includes **verbally** inflicting on a person:

— **Emotional pain**

— **Anguish**

and / or

— **Distress**

Emotional abuse can also be inflicted **non-verbally** on a person.

Examples:

— **Humiliating** a person

— **Intimidating** a person

and / or

— **Threatening** a person

All of this is awful, of course. And avoidable. You don't have to wind up in Fred's situation.

You can learn to manage the negative emotions — so that you can provide care with:

- **Acceptance**

- **Dedication**

and

- **Patience**

As long as you take care to manage your emotional stress, daily, caregiving can feel...

- **Manageable**

and

- **Rewarding.**

First: let's understand **what causes "emotional stress."**

Just like if you put a heavy boulder on a wooden table that's not designed to support it, this will place "stress" on the wood, eventually cracking the furniture.

Similarly, being in a caregiving role can place "stress" on your emotions and body.

The difference is, unlike that table, you have the capacity to improve the way you handle stress.

Also, unlike that table, you have the capacity to discharge your pent-up stress safely.

The biggest thing to remember about emotional stress ... is this:

It's not so much what happens to us that stresses us; rather, it's how we handle our experiences that determines whether we're stressed.

And if we let our emotions build up and get backed up, that leads to more stress.

SELF-HELP EXERCISES:

Here are three exercises to help you release pent-up stress.

— One, for when you're in public.

— Two, for when you're alone.

First exercise:

If you need to release anger and **don't have much privacy**, consider trying this:

Write down how you're feeling in a notebook.

Then tear up the pages (the tearing motion offers a good way to physically release the anger).

Second exercise:

If you have privacy, consider trying this:

Tie a knot on one end of a hand towel.

Pound a pillow with the knotted end of the towel.

At the same time, vent your anger by expressing how you feel, out loud.

You could try using words like the next three:

"I'm so frustrated." "I'm so frustrated." "I'm so frustrated."

"I'm so frustrated." "I'm so frustrated."

Or,

You could say anything else that comes to mind, **as long as you direct it towards the pillow**.

Keep in mind that you're not mad at the person for whom you're caring; you're frustrated by the challenges of caring for them.

That's why you're venting, safely at an inanimate object.

Or,

Consider trying this:

Third exercise:

Hold a small pillow up to your face.

Yell your frustration into the pillow (it muffles sound).

You can make a sound (groan / scream)

or

You can use words to vent how you feel.

After venting safely by using exercises one, two and / or three, caregivers typically find that it's much easier to be **accepting** and **understanding** of the person for whom they're providing care.

When your emotions aren't festering inside, it's much easier to be patient and supportive.

Next:

We'll explore a few resources to help you **keep managing your emotions, safely** — and also to

- Relax

- Laugh

and

- Have a little fun!

STEP 4

Find More Support

Here is an article that I've written especially for people in caregiving roles.

Taking Care of an Elderly Parent -- and Not Loving It? How to Turn Resentment Into Patience and Joy
— Published on The Huffington Post.

http://www.huffingtonpost.com/dr-suzanne-gelb/caregiving_b_5260566.html

Here is another article that is deeply personal and meaningful to me. The article contains my written responses to interview questions that I was asked.

The article is called:

True Story: I Helped My Friend Die Peacefully

http://www.yesandyes.org/2015/03/true-story-i-helped-my-friend-die.html

The "story" is about losing my best friend to cancer.

I was my friend's primary caregiver.

I learned so much from this experience as you can tell by this quote from the article:

"I also got to experience being a caregiver for someone who is terminally-ill as a privilege, not a burden. Ushering someone into the next chapter of life — or after-life, however you want to think about it — is an unforgettable experience."

On a lighter note…

I've also included some **fun resources**, too.

Like:

— Simple ideas to brighten your mood and make you laugh.

And, if you want to take the "fun factor" a step further…

I've also included some **exercises for you to try**.

Like:

— Creating a list of **music that makes you happy** and **movies that uplift your spirits.**

Doing things "just to have fun" is an important form of self-care!

FUN THINGS TO DO AND CHECK OUT:

Create a list of:

- **Soothing**, **relaxing** and **happy music** to **uplift** your day.

    Then, do an internet search to find some of that music and...

    Enjoy!

Create another list of:

- **Movies** you've seen (or want to see) that uplift your spirits

    Examples:

    Romantic comedies

    Love stories

    Inspirational stories

    Example:

    Stories that make the impossible seem possible

    Movies that show the best in people:

    Example:

    How a person's life can touch others, often in unseen ways

Watch this inspiring video **to** see:

- Beautiful, true stories about **unexpected generosity**.

Visit this <u>website</u> that will **warm your heart**:

- **The Daily Puppy**. (exactly what it sounds like!)

Or, if you're more of a feline person ...

Visit this <u>website</u> that's sure to bring a **smile to your face**:

- **The Daily Kitten**

IDEAS TO BRIGHTEN YOUR MOOD AND MAKE YOU LAUGH:

- **Read** the jokes and cartoons in your favorite magazine

    Examples"

    <u>Readers Digest</u>

    and

    <u>The New Yorker</u>

- **Reach out** to a friend who always makes you smile.

    Say,

    "Tell me some great news."

- **Play** with children and get some endorphins pumping — Examples

    Throw a Frisbee

Play catch

or

Just run around playing make-believe

- **Surround yourself** with positive words and art —

Example:

Like these inspirational quotes, chosen especially for caregivers.

- **Create** silly, new passwords for your various online accounts.

Why?

Every time you log in, you'll crack a smile :)

- **Take a look at** this short article from *Woman's Day* for 18 more ways to shift your mood.

Want even more support?

If you feel that you'd like some added support from a qualified professional such as a counselor or coach, don't hesitate to take that step.

You might even find a provider who will work with you over the phone or via video, from the comfort of your home — if that's something that you'd like.

My skill when working with people who want added support to manage the challenge and demands of caregiving?

— Helping clients **identify the negative feelings** they've been ignoring or unable to detect, and

— Some of **the reasons those emotions built** up in the first place.

During the course of our work together, clients discover:

— How to **release the emotional stress** that may be causing them to feel angry, sad or depressed,

so that

— They can **find pride and satisfaction in their work**, becoming **the best caregiver** they can be — while…

— Living the **healthiest, most joyous life**.

If you're considering seeking counseling, ideally, try to find a provider who is located in your geographical area, so that you can work face-to-face with that provider, when possible.

Remote sessions can be very convenient and effective. That said, in-person sessions offer an extremely powerful experience.

Perhaps you're wondering how a therapy session works?

191,885 people have been wondering - they viewed my article online on this topic. The article is published on my column, "All Grown Up," in *Psychology Today*.

The article is called:

What Really Happens in a Therapy Session?

Topics covered in the article include:

Choosing the right therapist, effectiveness of in-person therapy vs. phone or video format, and the value of seeing a therapist vs. talking to friends or family.

https://www.psychologytoday.com/intl/blog/all-grown/201512/what-really-happens-in-therapy-session

Next up in our Guide:

We'll talk more about **finding deep satisfaction in your work as a caregiver** — even when it feels **unpleasant** or **tough**.

STEP **5**

Find Satisfaction and Honor

We all want to be "helpful." We can all take pride in a "job well done."

And caregiving is one of the purest forms of "helpfulness."

Every action you take —

from

— sorting pills

to

— fluffing pillows

to

— cooking a meal,

to

— some of the less pleasant activities

Like:

— Cleaning up after an accident due to urinary incontinence

Is a deeply helpful gesture.

Creating a **loving, dignified environment** for the person you're caring for is **loving, dignified work**.

- **Focus on that.**

- **Find honor in that.**

- **Find satisfaction in that.**

FROM GUILT AND RESENTMENT TO COMPASSION, TENDERNESS AND APPRECIATION:

Here's a story about someone I worked with, who felt

- **deeply resentful**

about his position as a caregiver,

but managed to

- **change his perspective.**

Howie, 45, had been taking care of his 80-year-old father for almost a year.

*When Howie first learned that his father had been diagnosed with Alzheimer's disease, there was no question in his mind that his father would **move in with him**.*

*This meant **compromises** in:*

— his marriage,

— work life,

and

— other outside activities.

But Howie wouldn't have it any other way.

*"**Family sticks by family**," he said.*

*As time went by, however, Howie grew increasingly **resentful** —*

towards

- *his siblings who weren't helping him as much as he wanted,*

towards

- *his father for not being who he once was,*

and towards

- *the act of **caregiving** itself, because it **had turned his life upside down**.*
-

*Actually, he felt like he was **in over his head**.*

Feeling guilty for feeling resentful.

*When Howie came to see me, he was feeling **guilty** about his resentment.*

Acceptance.

I encouraged him to

*— **go easy on himself**,*

and to

*— **accept** how he was feeling.*

Insight and understanding.

I also pointed out that it wasn't his father who he was resenting,

*— it was the **situation** — the disease,*

and also

*— the **responsibilities** of caregiving.*

Release frustrations, safely.

I encouraged Howie to release his frustrations by doing two of the exercises noted in Step 3:

Recap:

First exercise:

— **Journal-writing** followed by ripping up the pages;

Second exercise:

— Pounding a pillow and **venting** at the same time.

Returning to love.

After Howie released his feelings, he remembered what his son, 8, had recently said to his grandpa:

"I'm so glad you're staying with us. I love you so much."

This reminded Howie not to take his dad for granted.

As he put it:

"I see now, what a beautiful opportunity I have to be compassionate and tender towards my dad."

"... To give back to him, and to grow and learn what's important in life.

But most of all it's a chance to give my dad a quality life."

This shift in perspective — from resentment to appreciation — opened the door to a much more meaningful caregiving experience for Howie.

Accepting help.

In time, Howie also found ways to share his caregiving responsibilities with others, and learned to accept help.

SELF-HELP EXERCISE — AFFIRMATION

The next time you're having negative feelings about your caregiving duties, try this affirmation. (fill in the blanks.)

Even though I don't enjoy doing

_____

_____

_____

I know that my actions are helpful, and that I am caring for {person's name} with so much love AND support. I can be proud of that.

Repeat that affirmation to yourself, as many times as you want to.

Feeling a sense of honor and respect for yourself, and the person you're caring for.

You might not feel instantly "overjoyed" about your caregiving duties, but you can find a sense of honor and respect — both for yourself, and the person in your care.

Next up:

We'll talk about how to take **extra-special care of yourself**, as you care for someone else. (It all starts with a plan!)

STEP **6**

Create a self-care plan

Everyone needs to build self-care into their day.

But…

As a caregiver, you need to treat yourself with extra kindness, because your responsibilities can be depleting.

If you don't tend to your emotions and your body, as we've talked about earlier in this Guide, you could become:

— brittle,

— angry,

— exhausted

and/ or

— just plain depressed.

And you could begin to direct those pent-up emotions towards the person you're caring for, which isn't helpful or fair.

So…

Take extra-special care …

to focus on self-care.

On the next page, you'll find a **planning worksheet** that can help you to **make self-care a higher priority**, every day, and every week.

SELF-CARE PLANNING WORKSHEET:

Create a worksheet for yourself, similar to the worksheet that begins on the next page.

You can make your worksheet via computer or by hand... whichever medium works best for you.

Then,

Fill the worksheet out with self-care practices that feel nourishing ... and realistic.

Example of a self-care practice that **might be** doable:

— Taking a 5-minute dance break while listening to happy pop music.

Example of a self-care practice that **might not be** doable:

— Signing up for a 12-week dance class with training 3 nights a week.

Put your completed worksheet somewhere visible, where you'll see it every day.

Like:

— On the refrigerator.

Ideally, fill out this worksheet once a week, **starting fresh**.

To keep things simple, write down **just one self-care practice** to try, for each category.

Don't overwhelm yourself with too many "assignments."

This is about **releasing stress** — not creating more of it!

Above all:

Treat yourself with kindness, patience and care.

When you're kind, patient and caring towards yourself…

This can help you to provide

- **Kindness,**

- **Patience**

and

- **Care**

to others.

THIS WEEK …

BODY:

To take better care of my body, I will

_____

_____

_____

_____

_____

_____

MIND:

To inspire and stimulate my mind, I will

_____

_____

_____

_____

_____

EMOTIONS:

To release pent-up emotions, I will

_____

_____

_____

_____

_____

_____

SATISFACTION:

To find honor and satisfaction in my work as a caregiver, I will

_____

_____

_____

_____

_____

_____

FUN:

And just for fun, I will

_____

_____

_____

_____

_____

_____

STEP **7**

Positive Submission

As a caregiver, things may often feel "overwhelming" and / or sometimes "out of control."

It may feel like you have limited "power" and few "options."

But as we explored earlier (when we talked about your "limitations") you actually have a considerable amount of power.

And you have quite a few choices.

For example,

You can:

— Choose to find safe, appropriate outlets for your emotions.

You can:

— Choose how to respond to frustrating, unpleasant situations.

You can:

— Choose to make time for extra self-care, instead of less.

But of course ... some things are **not** within your control.

Like:

— Whether your favorite doctor remains at the clinic near your home, or not.

Like:

— How fast your mother's broken bones will heal, after an accident.

Like:

— Whether your father will want to get better, or not.

Situations that are beyond your control...

When it comes to things that you cannot control, I often suggest to the people I work with that they:

— Cultivate positive submission.

Positive submission **isn't** the same as:

- "Surrendering"

or

- "Giving up."

It's a form of empowering realism.

It means saying to yourself:

"I'm doing everything I can, and that's all I can do."

FROM ANXIETY TO PATIENCE AND ACCEPTANCE:

This is a story about someone I worked with, who felt a lot of anxiety about being a caregiver.

By cultivating **positive submission**, she was able to provide care with more patience and acceptance.

When Sheri came to see me, her husband had been recently diagnosed with cancer. This was completely unexpected and she feared the worst:

"How could this happen, he's so athletic and full of life? I couldn't bear to lose him."

Sheri and Bob had been married for 20 years. He was her "life."

At 45, she couldn't imagine living without him.

Since his diagnosis, she'd been in shock. She was way past overwhelmed. Suddenly she'd been thrust into a caregiver role.

Her whole world had been turned upside down.

Just a week before, she had been a hard-working, highly successful, small business owner. All that changed, in an instant, with the diagnosis.

Since then, she'd been preoccupied with learning about cancer types and stages, treatment options, and dietary requirements for cancer patients.

But her every waking moment was filled with worry, fear and anxiety.

This affected her ability to function:

— Even preparing her husband's medications felt overwhelming.

— She couldn't relax.

— She felt tense and panicky.

—She was drowning in her fear of the unknown:

- *"How are we going to manage this battle? ...*

- *Do we need a second opinion?*

- *But we don't want to offend the oncologist? ... How are we going to pay the bills? ...*

- *How will this affect the kids? ...*

- *How is my husband going to cope? ..."*

Discharging fear, safely.

At one point during Sheri's visit with me, I explained to her that she needed to release her fear.

I then gave her a pillow to hold on her lap.

Next I suggested she close her eyes and visualize what she feared.

"Now hold the pillow gently up to your face," I said,

"And scream your fear into the pillow."

The pillow muffles sound.

(Just like a child would do if they were lost at the mall and couldn't find their parents, they'd scream: "Mommy!" or "Daddy!")

Calm and relief.

Once Sheri released her fear, she felt much calmer.

It's important to grieve.

She also cried about the fact that Bob was no longer healthy. She felt better after grieving the loss of his good health.

With her emotions feeling more balanced, we were then able to talk about "positive submission."

Making peace with reality.

This is a dynamic quality of our personality:

— the ability to submit to "what is," in a positive way ...

— the ability to move towards the acceptance of what is.

This doesn't mean:

- *being passive*

or

- *backing down,*
-

or

- *giving up,*

or

- *giving in.*

It means:

— ***Freeing ourselves*** *of the burden of bearing so much fear (in this instance).*

It means:

— ***Meeting life on life's terms,***

instead of

— *Being afraid of life or fighting what is.*

It means:

— *Trusting ourselves and whatever we believe in, to get us through life's tough spots.*

And it gives us the patience to hang in, and to embrace the moment.

Sheri resonated with this.

Instead of being afraid of losing her husband, or of not being able to cope, she mustered up the courage to be the best caregiver she could be— which included:

- ***believing in her ability*** *to give her husband loving care and support;*

and

- ***accepting the limitations of the situation —***

    knowing there were many things she couldn't control.

But she realized she didn't need to be fearful about that.

By embracing positive submission, Sheri realized that:

- **she could flow with life**

and trust that, no matter what,

- **she could love herself through any challenge.**

And, in the weeks and months that followed, she did just that.

SELF-HELP EXERCISE: SETTING YOUR INTENTION

The next time you're feeling **powerless** or **frustrated** by circumstances outside your control, try saying these words, aloud.

Or silently, in your mind.

— I will strive to make things better ... when it is possible to do so.

— I will vent my feelings safely and accept life's limitations ... when it is not.

As a caregiver, and human being, that is all you can do.

And that is enough.

A FEW FINAL WORDS

Making your own wellbeing a priority, prevents caregiver burnout.

Caring for another human being is a **privilege**.

Creating a loving, dignified environment for another human being is an **honor**.

And even if you're not feeling "terrific" about your role as a caregiver right at this moment, feeling stressed and perhaps even burned out (mental, emotional and physical exhaustion), you can learn to **manage the pent-up emotions** that may have been **building inside you**, and draining your energy.

Again:

You are not a table, forced to crack under the weight of a boulder.

You're a human being — dynamic, alive, with the capacity to:

- **Learn new skills**

- **Learn new ways to release stressful feelings**

- **Learn to change your perspective**

And

- **Learn to do things differently.**

Remember that, so that hopefully very soon, you can find more **meaning**, **satisfaction** and **pride** in your caregiving work.

And the person under your care can receive something priceless:

Love, patience and **care** — from **the best possible version of you.**

MORE TIPS, MORE TOOLS

5 FAQs about stressful caregiving situations and dilemmas.

Being a caregiver can be a nightmare — or a privilege. The choice is yours. Here are even more tips and tools to continue your journey to learn to tend to your own needs as you care for others..

Read on for my answers[1] to some of the more typical questions I've been asked over the past 3+ decades as I've helped caregivers who were feeling overwhelmed or burned-out, to **shift their perspective** and find **satisfaction** and **joy** in caring for another.

---

[1] The questions and answers are summarized here, to maximize your learning experience.

Question No. 1 — Parent's Declining Health

Understanding Why Talk and Touch Matters

My mom is in her 80's. She's always been well-mannered, helpful and loves to socialize.

About two months ago, we took her to the doctor because she started showing early signs of Alzheimer's (that's what her doctor explained).

Now she's uncharacteristically short-tempered and unpredictable. It's hard to watch. It's like she's not the same person she used to be.

This came on quite suddenly... I know she's old, but somehow I don't think one is ever prepared for this.

I've gotten used to her having problems related to aging — like arthritis, and a hip replacement that she needed.

But I think that when it came to conditions like dementia or Alzheimer's, in the back of my mind, my thinking was:

"Not my mom. This won't happen to my mom."

(Maybe that's like a young child who believes their parents are invincible.)

She lives with my husband and me at our home, but honestly, — and I feel guilty for saying this — we feel so helpless about this change in her personality that we tend to ignore her. I find myself thinking:

"What's the point in communicating?

Yes, she can still carry on a conversation with us, but what's the point if she doesn't follow-through with what we talk to her about because she's unpredictable?"

We've taken her to visit her doctor more often, lately. He doesn't talk to her much either... he just gives her medication and says she's depressed.

As much as ignoring my precious mother feels easy, my husband and I are beginning to feel really uncomfortable about this.

We both love my mother dearly, and we know what a special person she is / was, but short of turning back the clock, we don't know how we can be helpful to my mother if we can't count on her to always remember or follow-through on what we talk about.

From the bottom of our hearts we both want to help her.

How can we help her?

Response:

I can appreciate that your mom's declining condition comes as somewhat of a shock.

Even though, intellectually, we all know that losing one's faculties to a small or large extent is a possibility for an aging person, from an emotional standpoint it's not uncommon for an adult child of an elderly parent to think like you have:

"Not my mom. This won't happen to my mom."

It's important to grieve the loss of the fact that your mom, as you have known her your entire life (mentally competent), is not quite the same. This can help you to adjust to the reality of what is:

"You're still my mom. It's just that in some areas you're not able to function like you used to, and therefore you need more help.

It is my honor and privilege to help, any way I am able to."

It is possible to reach that place of **compassion**, **patience** and **empathy** within yourself, but only if you:

Allow your emotions (grief, in this instance) to be your friend (we don't tend to avoid friends) and embrace your grief by feeling it.

Then the grief will pass.

Why?

Because it will have served its purpose — to offer you a way to express how you feel... and in doing so, you are then able to transition from:

— What **was** (i.e., mom being mentally competent)

to

— What **is** (i.e., mom displaying some mental difficulties.)

If you find that you need some more help with processing your grief because it feels so deep, don't hesitate to reach out to a qualified professional.

Finding time to take care of yourself is vital to being the best caregiver you can be.

You may feel like you don't have time for another doctor's appointment, because you've been taking your mom to her appointments. That's understandable.

But try to do the impossible and find time to do this for yourself. It's likely to help you feel a lot better, and be an even better caregiver for your mom

When you love someone, it won't feel right to ignore them because of their limitations.

As to the discomfort that you and your husband feel about ignoring your mother, this reflects how much you both love your mother.

With love in your heart, it's understandable that ignoring another person because their capacity is limited, doesn't feel good or right.

So let's take a look at what you both can do to turn this around.

First, keep in mind that even though your mom is not always able to "follow-through with what [you and your husband] talk to her about because she's unpredictable," she's still a person who deserves to be treated with:

- **Dignity**

and

- **Respect.**

No doubt, being a caregiver can be frustrating and stressful, and this responsibility often triggers within us **a whole range of emotions** — from grief to anger, and everything in between.

When a caregiver is feeling some or all of these emotions and is stressed out (sometimes even burned out) by the responsibilities of caregiving, it's easy to lose sight of the fact that an ailing, elderly person for whom we're caring deserves to be:

- **Honored**

- **Appreciated**
-

and

- **Treated in a manner in which we would like to be treated.**

SELF-HELP EXERCISE: NUMBER 1.

Here's the first of two **self-help, writing exercises** that you may want to do, to keep yourself in check about how you're treating an ailing, loved one (i.e., your mom.)

Ask yourself the four questions below. Then **fill in the blanks** with your answers.

Try not to:

— **Overthink**

— **Overanalyze**

Or

— Let **guilt** cause you to **censor** your true response.

First Question:

Am I treating my mom in the way that I want to be treated?

_____

_____

_____

_____

_____

Second Question:

At night, just before I go to sleep, as I reflect on my day and the choices I made, do I feel good about how I treated my mom?

_____

_____

_____

_____

_____

Third Question:

Is there anything about how I treat my mom that I want to change or do differently?

_____

_____

_____

_____

_____

Fourth Question:

Do I respect myself for the way in which I treat my mom? If not, why not?

_____

_____

_____

_____

_____

_____

If you answered "No" to the first and / or second or fourth questions, and / or "Yes" to the third question, then you're ready for the second exercise that follows.

(Hint: Based on the details that you included in your question, I suspect that you'll be doing the second exercise that follows.)

Replace guilt and self-criticism with patience as you learn to be the best caregiver you possible can be.

Remember, this is a learning experience, so you can be the best version of yourself as a caregiver.

This means that there's no room for guilt and / or self-criticism for how you've treated your mom so far.

SELF-HELP EXERCISE: NUMBER 2.

Here's the second of two **self-help, writing exercises** to support you in becoming the best caregiver you can possibly be.

The four statements that follow can offer you an opportunity to change some of your behavior regarding how you treat your mother.

Fill in the blanks to any of the statements below that you feel apply.

By filling in these blanks, you are **consciously** and **sincerely** intending to **improve** how you treat your mother.

You can feel very good about your choice to do this.

First Statement:

From now on, I'm going to treat my mom as I want to be treated. This means that I will

_____

_____

_____

_____

_____

Second Statement:

At night, just before I go to sleep, as I reflect on my day and the choices I made, I will feel good about how I treated my mom because...

_____

_____

_____

_____

_____

_____

Third Statement:

I will change (for the better) how I treat my mom by doing the following things differently...

_____

_____

_____

_____

_____

_____

Fourth Statement:

I now respect myself for the way in which I treat my mom because I no longer [list "old" behaviors below]....

_____

_____

_____

_____

_____

Instead I [list "new" behaviors below]....

_____

_____

_____

_____

_____

Read these statements to yourself as many times as you want to, for as many days as you want to, until the new behavior becomes so **automatic** that it feels like second nature to you.

Why talk and touch can matter... a lot.

Growing older can be tough. Dealing with a decline in one's cognitive abilities, as with your mother, cannot be easy.

As such, it's not uncommon for an elderly person who is faced with this type of limitation to feel depressed and lonely — even if family is nearby.

Be kind, patient and loving

According to Mental Health America, over two million of the 34 million Americans who are 65 years or older are afflicted with some type of depression. Often, these symptoms are triggered by conditions such as arthritis and Alzheimer's.

This is why it is so important to talk to your loved one (your mother, in this instance), with kindness and with patience — regardless of whether it appears that she understands or will follow through or not.

Put yourself in her position for a moment... think about how much it would mean to you, if you were struggling with physical and / or mental limitations, to feel — even if just for a brief moment — that

— **You matter** to someone

— **You're important** to someone

— **Someone's interested** in you

— **Someone cares** about you

— **Someone loves you**.

And where appropriate, touch can mean so much to an ailing loved one… and can be so healing.

Touch can be calming.

Touch can let us know that…

— someone cares about us.

Ask yourself:

"Are we ever too old to enjoy our hand being held, or the comfort of a caring, loving hug?"

A simple gesture such as putting your arm around your mother's shoulder, can make a big difference to her — a small gesture of affection lets her know you love her.

Of course, talk to your mother's doctor and any other professionals that are involved with her care about any concerns you may have regarding her health and before making any changes to the care that you provide for your mother.

That said, the better care you take of yourself, by tending to your emotions and caregiver stress, the better care your mom can receive from you — a win-win for both.

Question No. 2 — Parent Won't Cooperate

Becoming Educated About Dad's Limitations

My dad is 79. He suffers from heart disease and arthritis, and cognitive impairment that his doctor says is moderate Alzheimer's disease.

The doctor says she is monitoring my dad every time we take him in for a visit, to see if the Alzheimer's is progressing.

My dad has always been controlling and he wants things his way.

The problem is that now he is so suspicious of everything that we do for him, or even that the live-in caregiver does for him — even when we do things exactly as he has always wanted them to be done (like how his shirts are folded after they've been washed, or how he likes his socks to be organized in his socks drawer after they've been washed).

Sometimes he gets mad when we do things according to how he has always wanted them to be done, and he thinks that we're out to get him — nothing could be further from the truth... we're just trying to follow his wishes.

I explain this to him — and he seems to understand — and sometimes even verbally agrees with what I'm saying. This leaves me to think that we've made headway, and that talking to him about this has solved the issue.

But... it's just a matter of time before he is suspicious again and honestly, kind of paranoid — like not in reality.

I'm so frustrated with this. What can I do to get through to him?

Response:

Your frustration is understandable and it's important to have a safe outlet to discharge this type of emotion.

Otherwise, you may:

React in an impatient way towards your father

or, in the extreme, you may

Explode verbally, and say things to him that you wish you could take back...

But can't.

[In this regard, readers of this Life Guide can refer to Step 3 of this Life Guide. That step is titled, "Manage Your Feelings."

In Step 3, you read about three self-help exercises to release stress, including anger. Unresolved anger and pent-up frustration can trigger stress.

My response to the question that was asked here, included suggesting similar exercises for safe discharge of pent-up emotion as the exercises that are included in Step 3.

As such, examples of those exercises are not repeated here.]

The power of knowledge.

You asked:

"What can I do to get through to him?"

Many people feel **helpless** when they find themselves in the type of situation that you describe.

They want desperately to "fix" the situation so that things go back to "normal" as know / knew it.

An important factor here, is to be sure to learn about the **nature** of your father's condition. This could give you greater understanding about what you appear to be describing as personality changes and changes in behavior… and how this may relate to his condition.

You could share with his doctor what you are observing in your father. Since his doctor has first-hand knowledge of your father and his condition, you could ask her for her opinion on what could be causing the behavior changes that you notice in your father.

You could ask your father's doctor for some literature or resources on the symptoms of Moderate Alzheimer's disease — and / or you might do your own internet search and see what you learn.

The point is that:

Being educated to a reasonable extent about the condition of the person whom one is caring for, can offer knowledge and insight.

Then...

- **things may not seem like such a mystery,**

- we may be **less likely to take things personally**,

and, therefore, able to be

- **more patient**

and

- **accepting**

of the **challenges** that the person we are caring for, is facing.

Question No. 3 — Caregiver Quits

Helping Caregivers To Be Their Best

My son is 52. He had a near-drowning accident years ago, and suffered brain damage because of this. He is good natured and has an endearing sense of humor, but he is also prone to muscle spasms, occasional seizures and loss of bowel control, among other things.

I don't have a medical background, but since his accident, I have learned to take care of him so that at night, I am his primary caregiver. During the day, other caregivers help out.

He works hard at trying to get things right - like trying to independently hold the forker spoon when he eats (most times someone feeds him,) or trying to lift weights (with some assistance to guide him) when he goes to the gym in our condo.

The problem is that sometimes he gets frustrated. Then he's verbally belligerent and, let's just say... not the nicest person.

I'm used to his ups and downs (some call it mood swings). And of course, I also knew him before his accident, so I remember what a sweet, good-natured person he was — and I still see glimpses of that now and then. So I don't take his belligerence personally.

But his caregivers during the day, seem to. We've had two in the past 5 months who both quit, and the current caregiver is also complaining about my son's moodiness. I'm worried she's going to quit. I can't afford professional caregivers, so these are laypeople.

It's a lot of work to go through the process of hiring a caregiver. How can I help them to see that my son is really a nice person?

Response:

Your love for your son and your appreciation for the person that he truly is, shines bright in the way you expressed your question. That is beautiful to behold.

That said, it's quite a dilemma that you find yourself in. For starters, it appears that because you're needing to hire non-professional caregivers (this is understandable because of your economic limitations) they are not sufficiently familiar with your son's condition so that they can recognize that his "belligerence" as you identify it, is not in reality, being targeted at them, specifically.

Instead, it would appear, based on your description of the problem, that his behavior is a result of his injury and consequent brain damage.

Communicate, explain and teach.

— You might want to try and **communicate** this to the caregivers. Don't assume that they know this.

Also, keep in mind that you've been close to this situation with your son for years. These caregivers haven't been exposed to your son and his condition for very long… relatively speaking.

— So you'll need to **explain** to them, with sufficient detail (but not to the point of overwhelming them), what to expect from him, and how his condition can even lead to personality changes.

This way, you can help them to understand his frustration and anger (at times manifesting as "belligerence") and to recognize that his behavior is not directed at them personally.

— Essentially, you're setting out to **teach** these caregivers how to cope with the very real challenges of caring for your son. ,

Caregivers can enrich the lives of the people they care for.

You can also tell them about some of your caregiving experiences with your son, if you'd like — and how you've been able to take such good care of him and enrich his life for all these many years.

This can give them some new ideas of things to try, when they feel overwhelmed with caring for your son — and his wants and needs.

Keep in mind that not all of the caregivers that you hire will have the temperament or the desire to "go the distance" and learn how to best serve the unique needs of your son.

Maintaining a positive mindset can go along way towards achieving our goals and objectives.

That said, keep a positive outlook and commit to holding an image in your mind of the type of person who would be best suited to care for your son.

Believe that it is possible to hire a person with these qualities.

Believe that you desire to hire a person with these qualities.

Next: A visualization that can help.

VISUALIZATION:

You'll need about 15 to 20 minutes for this exercise. Be sure that you won't be interrupted or disturbed during that time.

Go to a private space, preferably a room in your home.

Sit in a comfortable chair, or on the floor if you prefer.

Close your eyes.

Imagine that...

— you see a potential caregiver in front of you.

Imagine that...

— this person is deeply caring, confident and resilient.

Imagine that...

— this person prioritizes maintaining the dignity of anyone whom he cares for.

Imagine that...

— this person really wants to care for your son.

Visualize this person...

— in your home, caring for your son with the utmost respect.

Visualize this person...

— being friendly towards your son, and good company for him.

Visualize this person...

— being compassionate and empathetic when your son is frustrated... understanding why he is feeling this way.

Visualize this person...

— being someone who you can count on — and who won't buckle and want to quit because of emotional pressure.

Visualize this person...

— knowing other caregivers who would like to care for your son.

Visualize...

— hiring some of these other caregivers, as well.

Visualize...

the problem that you identified in your question being solved.

Appreciate...

— yourself for all you do for your son.

Appreciate...

— the privilege of caring for your son — and doing whatever it takes so that he can be well taken care of.

Question No. 4 — Caregiver Burnout

Learning To Avoid Your Breaking Point

My brother and I are caring for three parents — our mom and dad, both in their early 90s (bless them) and his father-in-law who is 82. They all live with us.

We have a big home, so fortunately space is not a problem.

Also, I am a freelancer and I work from home. This allows me to set my own hours, and create my work schedule around the demands of caregiving. All this is very helpful.

Here's where things get sticky:

My brother travels quite a bit. That means that I'm essentially left "holding the ball" as far as caring for these three elderly adults.

We do have some help that comes in to do some cooking and cleaning, but the bulk of the caregiving falls on my shoulders.

Oh, and I didn't mention yet, that I have two kids, ages 5 and 7, that are homeschooled. So that's another role that I fulfill.

Lately, I've been feeling exhausted... emotionally and mentally. I've also been having trouble getting restful sleep.

I went to see my internist for a check-up. He ran all kinds of tests and ended up telling me that physically I'm very healthy. But he cautioned me about the toll this stress could take on my health.

I think my efforts to try to be all things to all these people in my life is taking a toll on me. How can I manage my stress levels?

Response:

First, thank you for your dedication and for the care you provide to your parents, your brother's father-in-law, and to your own children. Your commitment to supporting others is admirable.

That said, unless you are in good health — physically, mentally, emotionally, and spiritually — it's going to be difficult for you to provide good care to your loved ones.

To avoid burnout, caregivers must prioritize their wellbeing and get the support they need with their caregiving responsibilities.

It's not uncommon for caregivers to focus more on the needs of others, than on their own health and wellbeing — and to not have the support that they need (physically, mentally, emotionally, spiritually and / or financially) to provide good care to a loved one.

The result: caregiver exhaustion and burnout.

Now let's get to your specific question:

"How can I manage my stress levels?"

A good place to start can be to identify if you are experiencing caregiver burnout. This is especially important because:

Caregivers often are so used to worrying and and being stressed about caring for loved ones that they don't always notice when they themselves are nearing exhaustion.

That said, some of the more commonly-occurring symptoms of burnout can include, but are not limited to:

— no longer enjoying things that you used to enjoy;

— difficulty concentrating;

— trouble sleeping;

— using a substance to help cope with feelings;

— easily frustrated or angered;

— physical ailments (e.g., headaches, neck aches).

You might want to do an internet search to learn more about the complete range symptoms that indicate caregiver burnout might be an issue, or you could check for resources at your local library.

Live-in caregivers would be wise to be mindful of the amount of hours they devote to caregiving.

Pay particular attention to how time-consuming your caregiving work is — keep a log of how many hours you are devoting to this.

Given that for all intents and purposes you are a live-in caregiver, you're likely to spend more hours in this role than if your loved ones to whom you are providing care weren't living with you.

Too many hours devoted to caregiving can impact caregiver health in a negative way.

This means that you need to be especially mindful of the amount of time that you are devoting to caregiving, making sure that you don't overextend yourself.

The role-reversal of being an adult child who takes care of a parent whose health is declining, can be stressful.

Add to that the stress of being an adult child who is caring for ailing parents, and the role reversal that this entails, and it's not hard to see how, if you don't prioritize your wellbeing, burnout could be on the horizon.

Another reason why it is essential for caregivers, like yourself, to do whatever they can to ease their stress levels, and bring back a sense of positivity and hope, is because even though:

caring for a loved one can be deeply rewarding, at the same time, it is also a long term challenge that can be disheartening.

Why?

Ask yourself these next two questions:

— Is there hope that that family members that I'm caring for will get better?

— Even though I'm really trying to do everything I can, is their condition worsening / deteriorating?

Many caregivers find themselves answering "No" to the first question, and "Yes" to the second question. As they look ahead to months and even years of caregiving responsibilities, they tend to feel disheartened by a future that looks bleak. This is stressful and drains them of joy and hope.

The good news is that:

Caregiver burnout can be avoided by prioritizing self-care, especially when it comes to managing your emotions.

Keep in mind that stress is not caused by any outer circumstances that we might be experiencing.

Stress manifests when we mismanage our emotions.

This is empowering because:

When we keep our emotions in check (so they don't build up inside,) everything feels so much more doable, and overwhelmed dissipates.

Why?

Because when our emotions are in check (i.e., not pent-up), then excessive fear (or another pent-up emotion such as anger or grief) is not clouding our ability to think clearly, and to problem solve.

When this type of fear (or other pent-up emotion) is absent, we have unfettered access to our **intellect** — the part of us that we rely on to fuel our ability to:

- think

- strategize

- organize

and

- make decisions.

But…

When strong emotions are present, these emotions can dominate and, in a sense, block our access to our intellect.

Have you ever heard someone say this next statement?

*"I'm so **mad**, I **can't think** straight!"*

That says it all — the emotion "anger" (***"mad"***) is blocking or clouding that person's ability to access their intellect (***"can't think."***)

That's when

— strong emotions such as overwhelm, panic and / or even depression, tend to consume caregivers.

That's when

— caregivers are especially vulnerable to feeling stressed.

That's when

— some caregivers may be very close to getting burned out, or in some instances, they may have reached their breaking point.

Create the opportunity to vent and express pent-up feelings, safely.

[Note to reader: At this point in my response to the caregiver, I suggested that she do some written exercises that were similar to the ones that you can find in:

— Step 1 ("What Are You Feeling?")

and in

— Step 2 ("What Are Your Limitations?")

of this Life Guide.

I then encouraged her to release her pent-up stress by engaging in self-help exercises that were similar to the three exercises (one, for when you're in public; two for when you're alone) that you can find in:

— Step 3 ("Manage Your Feelings")

of this Life Guide.]

Once you manage your emotions consistently, you'll probably find that other ideas for self-care will come to mind, so you can bring your best to your caregiving role.

These ideas may include:

— Asking family and friends to step in and give you a break.

— Incorporating some form of exercise into your day.

— Making time for some socializing.

— Making sure you're getting quality sleep and rest.

Your loved ones, who you are caring for, need you. But you have needs too.

Every caregiver has unique needs because every caregiving situation has it's own specific needs and challenges. So it's best that you assess your self-care needs and create a self-care plan to suit those specific needs.

Your plan is likely to change or be adjusted over time, as your caregiving situation and it's needs change.

So:

— **Be flexible** with your plan,

— **Be creative** with your plan

And most of all,

— **Be pleased** that your are learning to tend to your own needs as you care for others and making the choice to experience caregiving as a privilege — instead of a nightmare.

Question No. 5 — Role reversal

Embracing the New Role of Caring for my Dad

My dad is 79. He's had health issues for a while, and until recently I would visit him and check up on him every day at his home — where he lived by himself.

About 6 weeks ago, his doctor confirmed what I had already sadly begun to notice... my dad's mental faculties were gradually failing.

That's when I turned my life upside down, and I moved in with him, to take care of him at night (after I'm done with my day job)— and manage lots of things for him. There are assistants who come and help during the day.

It's not only caring for him that I do - I have to take care of his finances (like paying the mortgage and the people that help him during the day; and, keeping track of things to make sure there's enough money for his needs in the future). I also manage his healthcare (he has a lot of health issues), and deal with health insurance and bills. This is like a full time job.

I have two sisters. One lives nearby and helps when she can. The other sister is in another city. Sadly, she doesn't care about my dad - she's greedy and always wants money from him. Now she's questioning if he was competent when had his Trust revised last year. It's unpleasant and I had to get a lawyer for my dad, and he has to see more doctors because of this competency challenge.

I've never been a very emotional person, but what bothers me the most now is that I'm like "the parent" for my parent (my dad.) How do I get used to that?

Response:

Please know that you're not alone in how you feel. Especially in the early stages of beginning to provide care for, and to "parent" an an ailing, elderly mother and / or father, it's not uncommon for adult children who take on this caregiver role, to think things like:

"I can't get through this…"

Sometimes adult children are able to maintain their sense of humor and use this as a coping mechanism to handle some aspects of this difficult caregiving situation. At other times, things can feel nightmare-ish, like when these adult children feel overwhelmed and "out of sorts" because of the role-reversal (*"All of a sudden, I'm a parent to my mom or dad… and they're the child"*).

During these tough times, it can be helpful to write down whatever you're feeling and experiencing… about anything.

There are other safe tools that can offer a deeper emotional release and therefore greater relief; however, since you describe yourself as never having "…been a very emotional person," journaling can be a gentle but effective introduction to some emotional release.

Be sure to keep your writing **private**… and for your eyes only. This way, you can feel free to write whatever is on your mind and in your heart, without worrying that someone else might read what you wrote, and misinterpret it.

Try to be consistent with writing down your feelings. Do this daily.

Give yourself an emotional check-up at the end of each day — review how you felt during that day. If you felt anything unpleasant, that means: write about it before you go to sleep.

Expressing your thoughts and feelings by writing about them offers you a way to release some of that intellectual and emotional energy — otherwise it just accumulates inside you.

This can result in a build-up of emotions that might, at some point, erupt explosively.

Example:

— You might find yourself **yelling** at your dad, out of frustration … and then wishing you hadn't done that;

Alternatively, you might find yourself feeling:

— **lethargic**

or even

— **apathetic**.

One reason for this might be because you have so much pent-up, emotional energy inside you that it's causing you to feel drained and unmotivated.

Writing by hand in a journal offers unique benefits.

If possible, write in your journal by hand — it slows you down, giving you time to think.

I also find that that writing by hand seems to stimulate my brain, and I tend to be more involved with the power of the written word, rather than typing fast or not always staying focused on what I'm writing.

Also, if you're the type of person who spends many hours a day in front of a computer screen, you might enjoy the contrast of writing with pen and paper.

Establish a good habit — be consistent with keeping a journal.

That said, many people find typing convenient and easier. They also don't have, or want to, take the extra time to write. If that's your preference, than **digital journaling can be a suitable alternative**.

When all is said and done, what matters is do make a **habit** of journaling, and to do it **consistently** during those times when it's needed.

Caregivers would be wise to take action and reach out for professional support for their physical and / or emotional health, if they feel the need.

Becoming a parent to one's parent is a tremendous adjustment, and can take a toll on a caregiver's physical and emotional health.

Example:

As one adult child who was caring for a parent who has Alzheimer's explained:

"My mom sometimes says such hurtful things to me that should never be said. It's like she has no filter to screen out things that shouldn't be said.

These words (and sometimes her actions) are so hurtful to me — and what hurts even more is that when she talks to me like this, she's like a different person than the mom I've known my whole life.

It's hard not to take it personally and to be the "grown-up" in the situation."

This is why it's so important for caregivers who find themselves in this type of situation to make sure they have a safe outlet for their emotions.

After releasing their emotions safely and **always** outside the presence of their ailing loved one, these caregivers can feel:

- calmer,

- stronger

and

- more emotionally balanced.

Then hopefully they can resume their caregiving responsibilities, feeling calm and strong, and remembering that:

— Caring for an loved one is a privilege and an honor.

That said, don't hesitate to **seek professional support**, from a qualified healthcare provider, for your physical and / or emotional needs **if you feel the need to do so.**

Follow-up question: Afraid of messing up.

As I hear your answer (which makes a lot of sense, thank you), another question is in my mind — my dad always had very high standards for me. I know now that he meant well, but I think that when I was growing up, and ever since, he was always so critical of what I did. So I never felt like I did anything right, even if I got great grades and did well in sports, and later got a good job.

Now, as a caregiver, I'm so afraid of doing things wrong, of messing up, and being criticized by dad — even though, since his faculties are not so much under his control (and since I've moved into care for him) he hasn't been criticizing me at all.

It's like I'm the one who is not in reality, because in reality I'm not being criticized, but I'm afraid that will happen.

Response:

It's not uncommon that when there is a role reversal such as you are experiencing, things can get somewhat tricky, because while our biological parent is behaving in some ways like a child — and we're needing to step into the role of being a parent to our biological parent — the child who we once were, may be expressing him or herself via our emotions (e.g., fear in this instance.)

Since fear of criticism from your dad is something that you felt as a child, it's possible that some of that fear that you no doubt had to repress in the past, may be surfacing now.

Just being able to make this connection between what you feared in the past (i.e., being criticized by your dad), and what you are fearing now (i.e., being criticized by your dad), can be helpful.

Many people find that gaining insight and understanding as to why they are feeling the way they do, offers relief.

You might also want to do some journaling about this fear of being criticized.

Here's what one person who was raised in a critical environment said about the benefits of journaling about this:

"Even though what I was writing about was painful, my journal felt like a good friend — accepting, non-judgmental.

This was so comforting and healing for me. I felt relief from my anxiety and stress."

I hope that your journaling experience is equally positive.

WHAT'S NEXT?

Resources... To Keep Learning and Growing

I hope you've enjoyed this Life Guide. It is "technically" complete, but I wanted to give you some **more resources on caregiving and self-care** ... in case you'd like to continue the learning and the growing with me.

Here are some of my favorites — articles I've authored,[2] books I've written, and inspiring insights that I shared when I was interviewed by a reporter from the Weekend Today Show, to savor at your leisure.

Enjoy!

---

[2] Except where otherwise noted, all articles referenced in this section were published online.

CAREGIVING

Taking Care of an Elderly Parent -- and Not Loving It? How to Turn Resentment Into Patience and Joy
— Published on The Huffington Post.

http://www.huffingtonpost.com/dr-suzanne-gelb/caregiving_b_5260566.html

Family Caring For Family: When You Teach Your Children About the Geriatrics Needs of Their Grandparents, You Help Enrich a Unique, Loving Relationship
— Published in Hawaii Parent Magazine
(Focus on Learning Edition, October/November 1999).

The Art of Caring for Elderly Family Members
— Published in Hawaii Senior Prime (April/May 2004, pp. 19-20) (hard copy)

The Art of Caring for Elderly Family Members
— Published in Hawaii's Senior Lifestyles: The Newspaper for Hawaii's Seniors (Vol. V, No. 5 1988, p. 6) (hard copy)

Independence and Aging[3]
— Q & A published in Hawaii Senior Prime (November/December 2004, pp. 12) (hard copy)

---

[3] This is the subject of a question from a reader regarding caring for her mother at home. The magazine published the question, along with Dr. Gelb's answer.

SELF CARE

You Are The Best Investment You'll Ever Make
— Published in Dr. Gelb's column, "All Grown Up" on Psychology Today.

https://www.psychologytoday.com/blog/all-grown/201511/you-are-the-best-investment-youll-ever-make

6 Self-Sabotaging Habits You Need To Drop Right Now
— Published on Mind Body Green.

https://www.mindbodygreen.com/0-14014/6-selfsabotaging-habits-you-need-to-drop-right-now.html

The Greatest Cheerleader One Can Have — Lives Within: How To Stay Strong When Not Everyone Is Cheering for our Success.
— Published in Dr. Gelb's column, "All Grown Up" on Psychology Today.

https://www.psychologytoday.com/us/blog/all-grown/201902/the-greatest-cheerleader-person-can-have-lives-within

If You Want to Make Tomorrow Less Stressful—Start Tonight
— Published in Dr. Gelb's column, "Be Well At Work, on The Muse.

https://www.themuse.com/advice/if-you-want-to-make-tomorrow-less-stressfulstart-tonight

The Love Tune-Up: How to Amp Up the Love That's Naturally Inside You to Enjoy Happy, Healthy Relationships — A 14-Day Course That Can Change Your Life

https://amzn.to/2XQ7190

Welcome Home: Release Addictions and Return to Love

https://amzn.to/2vwXmIa

5 Ways to Stop Yourself from Eating When You're not Hungry — Published on Psych Central.

http://psychcentral.com/blog/archives/2014/10/30/5-ways-to-stop-yourself-from-eating-when-youre-not-hungry/

Learning To Feed My Hungry Heart: My Journey From Bingeing To Wholeness
— Published Dr. Gelb's column, "All Grown Up" on Psychology Today.

https://www.psychologytoday.com/intl/blog/all-grown/201904/learning-feed-my-hungry-heart

How to Succeed Everywhere: 10 Tips for Balance at Work, Home, in Relationships
— Written by Shelby Marra, published online on NBC's Today.

https://www.today.com/health/how-become-high-achieving-woman-work-your-relationship-parent-t33071

Side note: As my colleague, friend, and gifted writing teacher, Alex Franzen said: *"THIS IS AMAZING! Being interviewed by a reporter from NBC's Today Show? Uh, that's the big leagues!"*

Yes, that's what happened. Shelby Marra with NBC's Today Show in New York, requested an interview with me so that she could write this article featuring me, for TODAY.com's Successful Women series.

Stressed Out at Work? How to Cope -- Without Turning to Food or Booze
— Published on The Huffington Post.

https://www.huffpost.com/entry/stressed-out-at-work-how_n_6711034

How Successful People Do More in 24 Hours Than the Rest of Us Do in a Week
— Published on Newsweek; also published on The Muse.

https://www.newsweek.com/career/how-successful-people-do-more-24-hours-rest-us-do-week

Side note: The Muse is an online platform that attracts more than 75 million people each year, to help them be at the top of their game at work.

I'm honored to have received the praise below, from Adrian Granzella Larssen, Editor-in-Chief, in response to an article that I wrote for The Muse:

"Wow! This is fantastic stuff. You're clearly incredible at what you do, and I'm so thrilled to share your advice with our audience!"

ABOUT THE AUTHOR

Dr. Suzanne Gelb, Ph.D., J.D. is a psychologist, life coach and author. Over the past 3+ decades, she has helped people to learn to handle the challenges of caregiving and prevent or resolve caregiver burnout, using tools like the ones in this book.

Dr. Gelb's inspiring insights on emotional wellness have been featured on more than 200 radio programs, 260 TV interviews, and online on Time, Newsweek, Forbes, Psychology Today, The Huffington Post, NBC's Today, Positively Positive, Mind Body Green, The Muse and many other places, as well.

As a contributing writer to the Huffington Post, Dr. Gelb's first article was called, **Taking Care of an Elderly Parent -- and Not Loving It? How to Turn Resentment Into Patience and Joy**.

Dr. Gelb has taught workshops on various caregiving topics, including **"Role Changes for the Caregiver and the Care Recipient"** at the Hawaii Association Of Case Managers 17th Annual Conference (2004).

Dr. Gelb believes that it is never too late to become the person — or caregiver — you want to be. Strong. Confident. Calm. Creative. Free of all of the burdens that have held you back — no matter what happened in the past.

OTHER BOOKS BY THE AUTHOR

It Starts With You – How to Raise Happy, Successful Children by Becoming the Best Role-Model You Can Possibly Be. A Guidebook For Parents.

How to Get Your Kids to Cooperate and Help Them Become the Best Grown-Ups They Can Be. (A Life Guide.)

Helping Your Teen Make Healthy Choices About Dating and Sex. (A Life Guide.)

How to Get Ready to Be a Parent and Be the Best Mom or Dad You Can Possibly Be. (A Life Guide.)

How to Forgive the One Who Hurt You Most. (A Life Guide.)

How to Deal With People Who Drive You Absolutely Nuts. (A Life Guide.)

Aging With Grace, Strength and Self-Love. (A Life Guide.)

How to Navigate Being Single and Savor Your Dating Adventure. (A Life Guide.)

The Love Tune-Up: How to Amp Up the Love That's Naturally Inside You to Enjoy Happy, Healthy Relationships.

How to Rekindle That Spark and Create the Relationship and Sex Life That You Want. (A Life Guide.)

How to Find Work That You Love When You're Stuck in a Job That You Hate. (A Life Guide.)

How to Reach Your Ideal Weight Through Kindness, Not Craziness. (A Life Guide.)

Welcome Home: Release Addictions and Return to Love.

Real Men Don't Vacuum. And Other Misguided Myths That Cause Conflict in Relationships.

INDEX[4]

A

a privilege and an honor, 90
acceptance, 18, 33, 47, 49
accepting help, 35
Alzheimer's, 32, 56, 67, 69, 71, 89

B

breaking point, 78, 84
brighten your mood, 24, 26

C

care for others, 3, 55, 85
care for somebody else, 1
care for yourself, 1, 3
caregiver burnout, 53, 78, 79, 80, 81, 82, 98
caregiver role, 47, 84, 87
caregiving responsibilities, 35, 79, 82, 90
coach, 5, 28, 98
counselor, 28
create a list/worksheet, 25, 39

D

doing things, 24, 91

E

emotional abuse, 17
emotional stress, 16, 18, 19, 28
emotionally balanced, 90
empathy, 2, 11, 58
empowering realism, 46

F

"family sticks by family", 32
find more support, 23, 28
find pride and satisfaction, 28, 54
fun things to do, 25

G

getting restful / quality sleep, 78, 85

---

[4] The page numbers in this index refer to the printed version of this book.

H

have fun, 24
healthy outlets for your feelings, 15
helpfulness, 30
honor, 30, 31, 36, 42, 53, 58
how a therapy session works, 29

I

identify the negative feelings, 28
in-person therapy, 29
insight, 33, 71, 92
insight and understanding, 33, 92

J

"job well done", 30
journal-writing / journaling, 34, 87, 88, 89, 92

K

keeping a journal, 89

L

lashing out, 14, 15
learn to improve, 11

life coach, 5, 98
live-in caregivers, 80
loving, dignified environment, 31, 53
loving, dignified work, 31

M

making peace with reality, 49
manage the negative emotions 18
manage the pent-up emotions, 53
manage your feelings, 5, 14, 15, 70, 84

N

negative emotions, 15, 16, 18, 28

P

parent won't cooperate, 69
physical abuse, 17
positive mindset, 75
positive submission, 44, 45, 46, 47, 49, 51
positive words and art, 27
pound a pillow, 20, 34
privilege, 53, 55, 58, 77, 85, 90
process (your feelings), 4, 10

Q

qualified professional, 28, 59, 90

R

release frustrations, safely, 34
release pent-up emotions / feelings, 42, 84, 88
release the emotional stress, 28
releasing stress, 40
resources on caregiving and self-care, 93
responsibilities of caregiving, 34, 60
returning to love, 34
role as caregiver, 3, 6, 53

S

satisfaction, 28, 29, 30, 31, 42, 54, 55
seek professional support, 28, 90
self-care, 24, 37, 38, 39, 45, 82, 84, 85, 93
self-care plan, 37, 39, 85
self-care practices, 39
self-criticism, 6, 63
self-help exercise(s), 20, 61, 64, 70, 84
self-help, writing exercise, 61, 64
"spiritual training course", 2
stressful caregiving situations, 55

T

take care of yourself, 35, 59, 68
talk and touch, 56, 67
terminally-ill, 24
trusting ourselves, 50

U

unexpected generosity, 25
uplift your spirits, 24, 25

V

vent(ing), 20, 21, 34, 52, 84
visualization, 75, 76

W

writing exercise, 5, 11, 34, 61, 64

Y

your power, 11
your limitations, 10, 11, 44, 84
your limits, 11

www.ingramcontent.com/pod-product-compliance
Lightning Source LLC
Chambersburg PA
CBHW020143130526
44591CB00030B/193